WHOMERLEY WOOD MOAT
STEVENAGE

THE HOUSE
IN THE CLEARING

Philip Wadner

2015

Published by Cade Books

©2015 Philip Wadner

All rights reserved.

ISBN 978-0-9931987-0-0

Front cover illustrations - Key

1946 Ordnance Survey alongside Google Map Data ©2014 Google[15]	
Medieval Wagon, Thunderdell Wood, Ashridge ©2009 Chris Reynolds[43]	Cosmeston Medieval Village ©2010 Missy[49]
Moated Area Present Day ©2015 Philip Wadner	

This booklet is dedicated to our Labrador dogs
Mandy, Jenna, Biscuit, Sheri, Sophie, Ellie and Tessa,
who over the years have explored every part of
Whomerley Wood.

Acknowledgements

Thanks to Stevenage Museum for providing the photograph of their model, and to Chris Reynolds and to Missy for permitting the use of their photographs under a Creative Commons license. Also, I am indebted to the family of the late Delvine Beckley for allowing me to use her sketch of the moat.

Contents

Whomerley Wood Moat

The House in the Clearing

Rural England in Medieval Times

Life for the working classes was tough in England around the thirteenth century. Almost everyone lived in a rural area, and made their livelihood from agriculture. This was hard-earned because only pitiable yields were attainable from crops at that time, probably due to the poor quality of seed and the labour-intensive methods which had to be used for farming[1]. Largely unaffected by the Barons' wars, royal squabbles with Ireland, Wales and Scotland, and the Crusades, the majority of the population just got on with the business of day to day survival of the family.

Food was fairly basic, with most households growing vegetables in their own kitchen garden and baking with low grade flour from local grain. Except for the very poor, domestic livestock provided a source of meat, milk, eggs and wool[2].

For the average peasant, there was a fifty-fifty chance of dying before the age of twenty and even if one was fortunate enough to reach that milestone, there would probably only be a further twenty years or so remaining before the grim reaper called[3]. So, when compared to present day standards most people living in the thirteenth century were very young.

For a typical head of the household, the important benefit of being young was that the odds of remaining reasonably healthy were fairly high. Good health was essential, because he would be expected not only to produce sufficient income to pay rent to the lord of the manor who allowed him to reside on the land, but also to provide everything his family required such as a house, food, warmth and clothes[4].

Inhabitants of the myriad villages and hamlets across the country enjoyed some security through safety in numbers, but lone homesteads were exposed to local lawlessness and civil disorder. Some of these are known to have been surrounded by a water-filled moat.

It is estimated that the medieval period of history spawned some six thousand moated homesteads in England[5]. Most would have been sub-manorial since there were by definition far more of these than seigniorial sites where often lived the lord of the manor or at least someone holding high office or social status. Six thousand of anything doesn't sound an awful lot by today's reckoning, but should be seen in the context that the population of England around 1300 was only about 6 million, shortly to be halved by the Black Death (Bubonic Plague) in 1348. On the return of the plague in 1374, the population of the country was diminished further to approximately 2 million[6]. That is only around one quarter of the current population of London alone.

Stevenage

Conjecture has it that Stevenage was born in Saxon times, with settlers clearing areas of woodland and building their camps around what was to become the site of St. Nicholas Church[7]. This was the focal point of the village for the Saxons, probably because the site stood high above surrounding woodland. It was eventually to provide the Normans with a location for the Church where it stands today. A rapidly increasing populace through the thirteenth century resulted in the centre of the village migrating to the fork in the road where northbound travellers from Welwyn turned west to Hitchin or east towards Biggleswade. In an attempt to benefit from the wealth of those passing through, the village also expanded southwards, far beyond the original encampment[8].

The 1086 census, recorded in the Domesday Book, shows Stevenage being held by the Abbot of Westminster 'answering for 8 hides'[9]. A hide was the amount of land needed to support an average family and was typically about 120 acres. That made Stevenage around 1000 acres in total, or just 1.5 square miles.

Within 200 years or so, by the late thirteenth century, what had started out as a small settlement had grown from an insignificant village into a small town[10]. The rationale for this is uncertain, but was probably driven by its proximity to the major road carrying trade northwards from London. Local entrepreneurs doubtless saw an opportunity to make a living by selling services and goods to the increasing number of travellers. Stevenage was also granted a weekly market and annual fair in 1281 by Edward I, which resulted in its establishment as a central point of commerce for surrounding villages[11].

Whomerley Wood

Sandwiched between the chalk of the Chiltern Hills in the north, and the London clay of the south, the area around Stevenage was ill-disposed to agriculture[12] and without the development of modern farming machinery that would probably still be the case. Consequently, the region remained largely uncultivated and left to swathes of dense woodland until the Romans began deforestation in order to develop their settlements.

Approximately two and a half kilometres, or one and a half miles, almost due south of St. Nicholas Church there survives an area of ancient woodland known as Whomerley (pronounced locally as Humley) Wood. The present name is probably a derivation of Homeleys, a small tract of land, or more likely a sub-manor to use a medieval context, within the Stevenage area[13]. Many commentators suggest that the wood took its name from the Saxon words *ham* and *leah*, loosely meaning 'house in the clearing'.

An aerial photograph of the wood taken in 1950 shows quite clearly a footpath from the direction of Stevenage Old Town, which disappears into the woodland[14]. That same footpath is also plainly indicated on the 1884 Ordnance Survey map of the area.

Almost all of the footpath has long since disappeared under the roads and houses that make up the Bedwell area of Stevenage New Town. However, the path still exists from where it has been dissected by Six Hills Way, and is a popular entry point to Whomerley Wood. Across Six Hills Way, almost opposite to that entry point, is the junction with the aptly named residential street of Homestead Moat.

Curiously, the old path would have followed much the same trajectory as Homestead Moat, although displaced by about 100 metres to the east. It is fascinating to visualise the path traversing Six Hills Way, crossing the end of Badgers Close, and perhaps running through the rear gardens of houses in Abbots Grove. It would have met up with Bedwell Crescent around its junction with Cuttys Lane, where a 1946 map shows the footpath changing to a made up road leading to Pancake Corner.

By placing that 1946 Ordnance Survey map of the area alongside a current Google image, that same footpath can be identified on the map as it enters the north west corner of the wood. By looking closely at the tree patterns on the Google image, it is possible to see where the path continues into the wood.

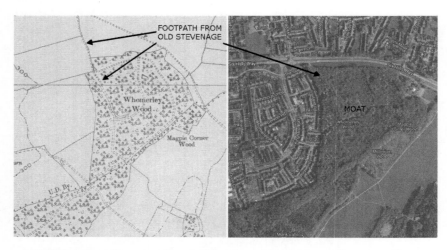

1946 Ordnance Survey vs Google (Map Data ©2014 Google, Stevenage[15])

Although the present path is contemporary, it may well follow the same route as it did in the thirteenth century or even earlier, perhaps as long ago as in Roman times. This is surely a coincidence, but if a line is drawn between the path and St. Nicholas Church, the trajectory between these two points follows very closely that of the old Great North Road from Welwyn before joining the Icknield Way on its route to Baldock, but displaced about half a mile to the east. Although tenuous and not overly convincing, the route of the path may fuel an argument that it existed in Roman times.

Much of the landscape was dense woodland, which would have made travelling a chore. However, if the footpath did exist along the whole distance, anyone living in the wood could easily have walked to the site of the old Saxon church in the centre of the original Stevenage settlement in less than one hour. The general direction of the path extended across the town is shown on the map below.

Moated Area to St. Nicholas Church (Map data ©2014 Google, Stevenage)

The Homestead Moat

About 200 metres along the path into the wood, on the left, there is a small causeway with a ditch roughly four metres wide falling away on each side.

Causeway Leading to Moated Area (Image credit: Author)

If the edge of this ditch is followed around, it soon becomes apparent that it was dug in an approximately square shape, some eighty metres along each of its sides, in the form of a moat. Actually, it should be more accurately referred to as a trapezoid, as none of the sides appear to be either the same length nor exactly parallel. Even so, most accounts of the moat describe it as square.

A lone voice, one Reverend H. Fowler, M.A. of the St. Albans Architectural and Archaeological Society wrote in 1891[16] that on a personal visit to Whomerley Wood he encountered a round area some 70 feet in diameter surrounded by a moat, with flint foundations about a metre thick following the ditch[17]. His mistake regarding the shape should be forgiven though, as from a position in the centre of the island much of the moat is difficult to distinguish. It does appear from that aspect that it could be more round than it is square, and indeed at the northerly corner there is a long curve which makes the ditch appear circular at that point.

As is so often the case, the truth lies somewhere in between the various accounts. Delvine Beckley reported on an archaeological study of the area undertaken in 1995[18], and included a drawing of the earthworks which appears to accurately represent the current shape.

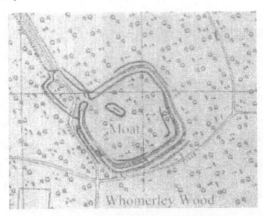

Sketch of the Moated Area (Image credit: Delvine Beckley[19])

Her sketch also indicates a second moated area between the causeway and the footpath, and this feature is included in a number of present day drawings. Indeed, a visit to the site clearly provides proof that it exists. However, medieval double moated areas were uncommon. It would seem that the only

9

reasonable explanation for having the conjoined moat here would be to give added security to the causeway leading to the island, but it would be surprising if that degree of protection would have been needed in the thirteenth century. On the other hand, the English Heritage entry for the site makes mention of a double enclosure for precisely that purpose[20]. Earlier records do not include any suggestion of a second moat, though, so there could be a tendency to believe that the extra trenches were dug in more recent times to connect the main moat with the ditches alongside the footpath to provide continuity of drainage.

Delvine Beckley's sketch also clearly shows the position of a pond on the island, and this is confirmed by a recent photograph taken about ten yards to the left of the causeway.

Pond on the Island from Outside the Moat (Image credit: Author)

10

It is possible that fish would have been bred in the pond, but since it is fairly small compared to the area of the island, it may simply have provided a convenient source of domestic water supply. In any case, the moat itself would have provided a far greater volume of water and so afforded a fine place to keep fish. The presence of two ponds has been recorded, but although that may have been the case in 1958[21], there is only one in evidence at the present time inside the moated area. A number of small hollows exist around the island which may contain water during prolonged wet weather, but nothing that might be described as a second pond. There is, however, a much larger pond in the wood on a north easterly bearing and approximately 130 metres from the moated pond. It is roughly rectangular in shape and measures some 15 metres by 30 metres.

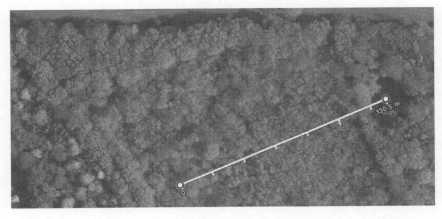

Distance Between Moat and Larger Pond (Map data ©2014 Google, Stevenage)

There appears to be no evidence to suggest the two pond sites are linked.

In the whole of the Stevenage area there are thought to have been only five moated homesteads. Two are in the manor of Stevenage itself, the second one being at Chells[22]. Although it is possible to speculate on why the moats existed, the answer has to be just that: speculation. Perhaps they were dug to safeguard the owner of the island from marauders, or possibly to protect from civil commotion. Maybe to offer some defence against an invading army, or provide sanctuary from disease. Possibly to keep out wild animals, or keep in domestic ones, or even incorporated as a design feature as an alternative to hedges or walls.

Most wild animals that could pose a threat to a family living apart from the main settlement area, such as wolves, boar and perhaps even bears, had more or less become extinct through being hunted in this part of England by the thirteenth century[23]. However, even the presence of the few remaining, or perhaps foxes, or the ostensibly innocuous deer would probably have played havoc with food stores (both those for the family and for their animal stock). Clearly a moat would have protected against such raids, but so would a thick hedge or fence.

Rural Hertfordshire in the thirteenth century was a relatively peaceful place to live, with only minor disputes over land boundaries and arguments about entitlement to tithes. Invasions by Romans, Angles, Saxons, Jutes and Vikings were long consigned to history, and the population of Stevenage was far enough distant from battles between King John's royalists and rebel barons over interpretation of the Magna Carta and its effect on the King's power over the law of the land for them not to be of any great concern[24]. However, with its close proximity to increasingly busy trade routes, it would be most surprising if outlaws and bandits were in short supply. The wooded areas south of the town, especially those close to what would become the Great North Road, would have been ideal places for bands of robbers and fugitives to congregate and hide. So, the moat in Whomerley Wood may well have been dug to offer a line of defence against such marauders.

The Black Death was not to reach Stevenage until 1349[25], and the moat is understood to predate this by at least around a century. However, there were no modern medicines at the time which meant that common infections and diseases such as dysentery, gonorrhoea, typhoid, and even measles and influenza could inflict a devastating blow on the population[26]. By digging a moat, the occupier of the island could have exercised at least some control over who was permitted entry and allowed close contact with the family, but this seems an unlikely reason given the amount of effort which would have been involved.

In some instances, it is possible that drainage was a major incentive, especially in areas of heavy clay soil such as Stevenage. In the case of the Whomerley Wood moat this could well have been the primary motivation. Even today, drainage in the wood is a significant problem, with paths and tracks quickly becoming waterlogged after just a few days of moderate rainfall. Small culverts recently dug to assist with moving the water away from public footpaths soon become full, taking many days to clear. Certainly, come autumn most years the moat is starting to fill up if it hasn't already done so during a wet summer. With its close proximity to Fairlands Valley, and the likelihood that the water table in that area was higher in medieval times[27], drainage was probably an even greater challenge than it is today. The presence of a moat around the homestead would have gone a long way towards solving that problem.

So, although it is exciting to associate the moat with a form of fortification, there is no nearby water source to ensure it was kept filled. It is perfectly feasible, therefore, that it may have been dug for a far more mundane purpose such as drainage, or simply in recognition of the social status of the resident.

Habitation

In 1925, archaeologist Margaret Murray from the University of London supervised an excavation team and discovered items of medieval household pottery at the moated site[28]. In 1953, Heinz Bosowitz, a bricklayer with an interest in archaeology and working on the New Town development, unearthed some 1,000 fragments ranging from crude tools to floor tiles[29]. However, no modern day investigations so far have confirmed that there was a building on the site.

Of course, it must not be forgotten that archaeological finds as far back as the Romans have also been discovered there[30]. This invites the prospect, even if an unlikely one, that the moat may have been dug in the four centuries between Caesar's armies landing on our shores and then abandoning any attempt to continue colonisation. Perhaps it was dug at some time through the Dark Ages, or maybe during the rise of Anglo Saxon settlement. Indeed, perhaps it existed before any of those.

Although there appears to be only circumstantial evidence, the island within the moat is suggested by many historians to have been the location of a thirteenth century homestead belonging to the de Homeleys. Their family name would almost certainly have been taken from the Stevenage sub-manor of Homeleys. However, there is more than one scholarly suggestion that it was the manor which took its name from the family[31], and there are indeed instances where freemen have negotiated to rent large tracts of land directly from the owner[32]. It has to be remembered, though, that if there was a clearing and perhaps buildings of some sort existing there in Saxon times, they could pre-date the de Homeleys by many centuries. Ivo de Homeley (Homle, Homlie, Homele) held 140 acres (about 0.25 square miles) of land in the manor of Stevenage in 1275[33], and Ralph de Homeley is recorded in the Lay Subsidy Rolls for Hertfordshire in 1293[34].

Homeleys was owned by the Abbot of Westminster to whom it is said to have been granted by Edward the Confessor in 1066[35]. Although the de Homeleys may not have owned the area of land in a literal sense, for Ralph de Homeley to appear in the Lay Subsidy Rolls he must have been sufficiently wealthy to be one of just seventy four Stevenage men who were directed to pay subsidy taxes. However, he is no longer included in the returns for the year 1307[36].

There is an entry from the 1307 Lay Subsidy Rolls for one William le Homles who was charged 8½d, a seemingly small amount but noteworthy compared to the total taken for Stevenage of £4-12s-10d[37]. Given the vagaries which affected the collection of census data many centuries later, it is quite possible that William le Homles was actually a de Homeley. Nobody with that or a similar name is listed in the returns for 1334 anywhere in the Broadwater Hundred, so it would appear that by 1334 the family had either moved out of the locality or were no longer considered sufficiently wealthy to pay tax. Alice

Homeley is thought to have held the sub-manor at some point after Edward III took the throne in 1327[38].

It is reported that in 1357, one John Homlie was brought before the Stevenage manor court accused of poaching rabbits[39]. That is not to say, though, that John Homlie had little wealth. It could perhaps have been more a sign that life in Stevenage around that period was humdrum to the extent that catching rabbits offered a highlight to the working week.

It seems probable from his given name that Ivo de Homeley had a strong Norman ancestry. Thought to have Teutonic origins, and to have been introduced into England only after the Norman Conquest, the element *iv* means 'yew' so the name Ivo may, therefore, have related to an archer's bow. The name is rare in present day England, although the French version *Yves* is still popular. Ralph (Ralf) was also a very fashionable name in the thirteenth century, again with Norman connotations and it goes without saying that the given name William has an even stronger association with the Normans.

The social status of Ivo and probably Ralph de Homeley makes it difficult to predict their spoken language. The Norman invasions succeeded in erasing almost all Anglo-Saxon vocabulary, and French continued to be used by the ruling classes and most of the clergy into the early thirteenth century. This was not the case though for the lower classes, who had continued to use their English regional dialects. This was not a stubbornness towards change, but simply because nobility and the working classes didn't have much to do with each other. By 1275, English was once again becoming the dominant language spoken by all social classes. However, the influence of French vocabulary and pronunciation on 'Old English' continued well into the fourteenth century and it seems likely that the de Homeleys would have been caught up in a puree of different lexis[40].

Transport

Unlike in today's way of life, there was no need for the average agricultural worker to be able to travel much further than they could walk. This was just as well, because walking was the only option for most people in the thirteenth century. Apart from getting to and from the fields in which they laboured, a trip to the nearest village to buy or sell essential goods would have been just an occasional outing.

Anyone sufficiently wealthy would have owned a horse, and this would have increased the distance which could be travelled to about thirty or forty miles in a day at a brisk walking pace. In an emergency, the distance could be doubled at a canter and with frequent rest breaks. For carrying goods, pack horses would have been used, but being limited to walking pace could not have covered anything like those distances.

With 140 acres of land to cultivate, and possibly having access to what is now Fairlands Valley to use as pasture for their livestock[41], the de Homeleys would probably have possessed a horse or two, although there are only fourteen recorded in the entire Stevenage manor in 1273[42]. In all likelihood, they would also have owned, or had ready access to, at least one cart, and perhaps a four-wheeled wagon as well, each pulled by a horse or maybe an ox diverted from the task of ploughing if the going was tough[43].

Medieval Wagon, Thunderdell Wood, Ashridge (Image credit: Chris Reynolds[44])

Animal feed would have to be moved around, crops gathered from the fields, produce and livestock taken to market and maybe the occasional family treat of an excursion to the nearest large town. Also, a considerable amount of travel may have been involved carrying produce to the Westminster land owner to satisfy the Abbot's bailiffs[45].

There were no made up roads, just dirt trails between major locations. Tracks or drags existed around the perimeter of fields, and perhaps wider droves where movement was a regular occurrence. They would all have been difficult to negotiate in wet weather, and uncomfortably rutted in the dry seasons.

Manor House, Homestead or Farm

The moated building, or group of buildings, is referred to in the literature as a homestead, farmstead, manor, manor house, even 'moated and fortified manor house'[46]. Precisely what form the building(s) took, if indeed any existed, would have depended largely upon the social status of the owner[47].

Since there is a strong consensus among commentators that the de Homeleys resided on the island within the moat, it is a fascinating exercise to speculate how it may have appeared to a traveller passing through the wood.

Further guesswork is needed, however, regarding the size of the family. It is also possible that agricultural workers and maybe general labourers who were not necessarily related also lived within the constraints of the moated area.

Whether the de Homeley family was large or small is open to supposition, but with an average age of the population around twenty one, it has been hypothesised that the typical family size for the period was surprisingly low, at only 3.5[48]. However, economic and social status would have had a positive influence on the de Homeley family numbers, potentially affording them an advantage over much of the population. For example, the incidence of child mortality may have been lower for them as they might have been able to afford the services of a physician, and it could well have been possible for the household to support ageing relatives who, in poorer families, might not have survived. On balance, it is quite possible that the nuclear family may have numbered six or more. Perhaps de Homeley, his wife, an ageing parent and maybe three children.

The area enclosed by the moat is about one and a half acres, so there is plenty of room for more than a single building even taking account of the pond. A villein and his family, who would have worked the lord's land in return for a small area of their own, might have lived in a simple one-roomed house little more than a hut constructed from wood and straw.

A family slightly higher on the social scale may have been able to afford a basic cruck-framed house with wattle and daub walls perhaps set into stone foundations[49].

However, with 140 acres to their name, the social status of the de Homeley family was above that of a common peasant. It is quite likely they owned more than one building and that their home took the form of a group of structures.

Cosmeston Medieval Village (Image credit: Missy [50])

A medieval house on a grander scale would have been built of stone, and may have had an upper floor for sleeping arrangements. The owner would probably have been able to afford glass in the windows, perhaps a chimney, and a tiled roof.

Even though the de Homeleys may have aspired to such heights, it seems clear from the site that any building inside the moat must have stopped very short of being an imposing 'manor house' of the type traditionally thought to be fit for a lord.

A visitor to Stevenage Museum would have the pleasure of viewing a model of the moated enclosure, created by the curator at the time. It includes a large wooden cruck-framed house, almost a hall, with what might be wattle and daub walls, and a thatched roof with a central hole blackened by smoke from the fire.

Model of the Moated Enclosure (Image credit: Stevenage Museum[51])

The building looks as though it could easily accommodate six people, perhaps more than that number if there are raised structures inside for sleeping arrangements. Often this main building would also have provided shelter for domestic animals, perhaps a few cattle, goats, or pigs. However, a second structure has been included within the museum model, lower in stature but of similar construction, which might be there to provide shelter for domestic animals. A third, much smaller, building could perhaps be a store of some kind.

Summing up...

There is very little information published about the Whomerley Wood moated homestead, and each source carries scarce detail. The archaeologist Margaret Murray said in 1926 at a talk to Stevenage residents about her excavations in the wood, that more is known about the time of Moses than about the people of Stevenage in medieval times[52]. That sentiment still rings true to the present day.

Even so, by knitting together morsels of fact with scraps of circumstantial evidence, a reasonable conclusion may be reached that the moated area indeed contained a number of buildings that were occupied by the de Homeley family around the turn of the thirteenth century.

There appears to be an excellent chance that the Stevenage Museum model represents closely what stood on the island, but without further excavation at the site and the discovery of evidence such as post holes or maybe foundations or wall remnants, nobody can know for sure what buildings existed there. Certainly, if the homestead structures had walls of stone or brick, they would have required substantial foundations which are likely to have survived in some form to the present day.

Regrettably, until archaeologists and local historians explore further, we can do no more than daydream about the people who lived at the house in the clearing, and wonder at the secrets whispering amongst the trees now standing in their place.

> **Please remember that the moated site is an English Heritage Monument and that unauthorised excavation is not permitted.**

Time Line - Whomerley Wood

43-400	Roman presence indicated by discovery of Samian and other pottery fragments
100	Romano-British family, probably wealthy, farmed near the wood, and built the Six Hills burial mounds[53]
450-1000	The Dark Ages
1086	Manor of Stevenage recorded in the Domesday Book
1275/93	de Homeleys resident in the manor of Homeleys, probably at the moated homestead
1349	Black Death reached Stevenage
1400	Homeleys held by John Chertsey of Broxbourne[54]
1413-22	Wood recorded as Homleye, then Homlefeld[55]
1616	Free warren in Homeleys granted to William Lytton[56]
1836	Tithe Map of Stevenage shows Whomerley Wood, Whomerley Nook, Six Acres Homeleys and Ten Acres Homeleys [57]
1920s	Accounts in The Times (London) of fox hunting taking place through Whomerley Wood
1925	Excavation at the moated site by Margaret Murray unearthed medieval pottery fragments
1946	Woodland threatened by the New Town Act
1950s	Path from Old Stevenage entering Whomerley Wood in north west corner lost under new buildings in Bedwell, and intersected by Six Hills Way
1953	Excavation at the moated site by Heinz Bosowitz (unauthorised) unearthed 13th/14th century pottery and animal bones
1991	Moated site scheduled under English Heritage as an Ancient Monument
1995	Historical and field survey carried out, indicating some features dating from Romano-British period

Finally, folklore has it that...

... there is link between Whomerley Wood and the six barrows on the Great North Road approaching Stevenage. The Devil, in a roguish mood, was one day sitting at the edge of Whomerley Wood watching people walking along the road. Becoming bored, he took a shovel and used it to dig a hole in the wood and threw the soil at passers-by. Six times he did this, those six heaps of soil still laying in a row at the side of the road for all to see. A seventh shovelful was dug, but the handle broke and the clod of earth flew wildly off course and hit Graveley Church, knocking off the steeple.

... the spectre of an evil-looking black dog has been recorded haunting the Whomerley Wood area[58]. The dog is said to have been huge, perhaps the size of an ass, with its head bowed to the ground and its tail curled over its curved back. It has been said that the black dog was thought to be a representation of the Devil.

... a monastery existed in Whomerley Wood, and it was this building which was later occupied by the de Homeleys[59].

References

[1] Sommerville, J.P. (2013) *Medieval English Society* [Online]. Available at http://faculty.history.wisc.edu/sommerville/123/123%2013%20Society.htm (Accessed 30 November 2014)

[2] Vaasjoki, Susi(2001) *Food and Drink in Medieval England* [Online]. Available at http://www.ling .helsinki.fi/~vaasjoki/exlibris/medfood.html (Accessed 29 November 2014)

[3] Mortimer, Ian (2009) *The Time Traveller's Guide to Medieval England*, London, Vintage Books, 35

[4] King, Gareth (2011) 'The 13th Century Manor House', *Keyworth and District Local History Society* [Online]. Available at http://www.keyworth-history.org.uk/about/reports/1101.html (Accessed 30 November 2014)

[5] Walker, J.S.F. and Tindall, A.S. (1985) 'The Moated House', *Country Houses of Greater Manchester*, Manchester, GMAU, 62

[6] Medieval Combat Society (2013) 'The Black Death', *Historical Information* [Online]. Available at http://www.themcs.org/black%20death.htm (Accessed 30 November 2014)

[7] Trow-Smith, Robert (1958)*The History of Stevenage*, Kendal, The Stevenage Society, 4

[8] Ashby, Margaret (1982) *The Book of Stevenage*, Buckingham, Barracuda Books, 43

[9] Morris, John (1976) 'History from the Sources', *Domesday Book - Hertfordshire*, Chichester, Phillimore, 135b

[10] Ashby, Margaret (1982), 12

[11] Trow-Smith, Robert (1958), 12

[12] Niblett, Rosalind (1995) Roman Hertfordshire, Wimborne, Dovecote Press, 9

[13] Trow-Smith, Robert (1958), 10

[14] Ashby, Margaret (2004) *Stevenage Streets*, Stroud, Tempus Publishing Limited, 81

[15] National Library of Scotland (2014) *Historic Map Images Side by Side* [On line]. Available at http://maps.nls.uk/geo/explore/sidebyside.cfm#zoom=16&lat=51.90127&lon=-0.18939&layers=171 (Accessed 9 December 2014)

[16] Fowler, H (1891) *The Six Hills, Stevenage* [On line]. Available at http://www.stalbanshistory .org/documents/1890_1891_06_.pdf (Accessed 8 December 2014), 40

[17] ibid., 42

[18] Beckley, Delvine (2002) *Monks Wood and Whomerley Wood, An Historical and Field Survey in Stevenage*, Hertfordshire's Past Number 53, Hertford, Hertfordshire Archaeological Council

[19] ibid.

[20] English Heritage (1991) *Whomerley Wood Moated Site* [On line]. Available at http://list.english-heritage.org.uk/resultsingle.aspx?uid=1012052 (Accessed 20 December 2014)

[21] Trow-Smith, Robert (1958), 14

[22] Stevenage Borough Council (2014) 'Settlement in the Stevenage Area in the Medieval Period', *About Stevenage* [Online]. Available at http://www.stevenage.gov.uk/about-stevenage/museum /47012/30115/30181/ (Accessed 5 December 2014)

[23] Magnusson, Halldor (2013) *Availability of select wild animals in Britain during the early Medieval* [On line]. Available at https://halldorviking.wordpress.com/2013/06/14/availability-of-select-wild-animals-in-britain-during-the-early-medieval/ (Accessed 5 December 2014)

[24] Wikipedia (2014) *History of Hertfordshire* [Online]. Available at http://en.wikipedia.org /wiki/History_of_Hertfordshire (Accessed 6 December 2014)

[25] Ashby, Margaret and Hills, Don (2010) *Stevenage, A History from Roman Times to the Present Day*, Lancaster, Scotforth Books, 11

[26] La Belle Compagne (2014) *Medieval Diseases* [On line]. Available at http://www.labelle.org /top_diseases.html (Accessed 6 December 2014)

[27] Fisher, D (u.d.) *Fairlands Valley Park*, Stevenage, Stevenage Borough Council, 3

[28] Stevenage Museum, Cuttys Lane, Stevenage

[29] ibid

[30] Trow-Smith, Robert (1958), 6, 14

[31] Page, William (ed.) (1912) *Broadwater Hundred*, 'The Victoria History of the County of Hertford' [On line]. Available at http://www.mocavo.com/The-Victoria-History-of-the-County-of-Hertford-Volume-3-2/856322/251 (Accessed 25 December 2014)

[32] Mortimer, Ian (2009), 49

[33] Page, William (ed.) (1912), 'Stevenage Manors - Homeleys', *British History Online* [Online]. Available at http://www.british-history.ac.uk/report.aspx?compid=43593 (Accessed 4 December 2014)

[34] Trow-Smith, Robert (1958),14 [Lay Subsidy Rolls for 1293 are unpublished in modern form]

[35] Trow-Smith, Robert (1958), 8

[36] Brooker, Janice (1998) (ed.) 'Hertfordshire Lay Subsidy Rolls 1307 and 1334', *Stevenage*, Hertford, Hertfordshire Record Society

[37] ibid

[38] Page, William (ed.) (1912) *Broadwater Hundred*.

[39] Trow-Smith, Robert (1958), 30

[40] Mastin, Luke (2011) The History of English [On line]. Available at http://www.thehistoryofenglish.com/history_middle.html (Accessed 17th January 2015)

[41] Fisher, D (u.d.), 3

[42] Trow-Smith, Robert (1958), 19

[43] Langdon, John (1982) *The Economics of Horses and Oxen in Medieval England* [On line]. Available at http://www.bahs.org.uk/AGHR/ARTICLES/30n1a3.pdf (Accessed 6 January 2015), 31

[44] Reynolds, Chris (2009) *Another view of the Medieval Wagon, Thunderdell Wood, Ashridge*, Geograph, Creative Commons Share Commercial, Attribution, Adapt [On line]. Available at http://www.geograph.org.uk/photo/1387232 (Accessed 6th January 2015)

[45] Trow-Smith, Robert (1958), 18

[46] Ashby, Margaret and Hills, Don (2010), 8

[47] Trow-Smith, Robert (1958), 14

[48] Krause, J (1957) *The Medieval Household: Large or Small?* [On line]. Available at http://onlinelibrary.wiley.com/doi/10.1111/j.1468-0289.1957.tb00673.x/abstract (Accessed 18 December 2014)

[49] MacDonald Educational (1977) *Medieval Life - Housing* [On line]. Available at http://www.historyonthenet.com/medieval_life/houses.htm (Accessed 28 December 2014)

[50] Missy (2010) *Cosmeston Medieval Village*, Flickr, Creative Commons Share Commercial, Attribution, No Derivatives [On line]. Available at https://www.flickr.com/photos/missy-and-the-universe/4319423844/ (Accessed 7 December 2014)

[51] Stevenage Museum, Cuttys Lane, Stevenage

[52] Unknown (1926) 'Finds in a Wood', *Miss Murray and Stevenage Discoveries*, Hertfordshire Express 23 January 1926

[53] Ashby, Margaret and Hills, Don (2010), 1

[54] Page, William (ed.) (1912) *Broadwater Hundred*, 143

[55] DEEP (2014) *Whomerley or Humbly Wood*, 'The Historical Gazetteer of England's Place-names' [On line]. Available at http://placenames.org.uk/browse/mads/epns-deep-15-c-mappedname-001683 (Accessed 28 December 2014)

[56] Page, William (ed.) (1912) *Broadwater Hundred*

[57] Pitcher, June (1990) A *Sketch Map of Stevenage in 1836*, Stevenage, The Stevenage Society for Local History,12,13

[58] Knibb, Ashley (2013) *The Black Shuck* [On line. Available at http://ashleyknibb.com/category/research/cryptozoology/the-black-shuck/ (Accessed 20 December 2014)

[59] Holton, Richard (2007) *Shephall Manor Other Records* [On line]. Available at http://www.shephallmanor.net/chapter_7.htm (Accessed 8 December 2014)

NOTES

Printed in Great Britain
by Amazon.co.uk, Ltd.,
Marston Gate.